# Echoes Of Bharat

## A Poetic Journey through time

Hemant Avhad

BookLeaf Publishing

India | USA | UK

Made with ❤ on the BookLeaf Publishing Platform
www.bookleafpub.in
www.bookleafpub.com

# Dedication

To Bharat Mata,
Whose sacred soil has nurtured sages, warriors, and
dreamers alike.
Whose rivers flow with wisdom, and whose mountains
stand as sentinels of time.

To the brave hearts who bled for her freedom,
To the wise minds who shaped her destiny,
To the unsung heroes whose sacrifices remain etched in
eternity.

To every soul who carries Bharat in their heart,
Who walks the path of Dharma,
Who dreams of a glorious tomorrow,
And who believes in her eternal rise.

This book is a tribute—
A song of valor, wisdom, and sacrifice,
An ode to the spirit that never breaks,
A testament that Bharat shall shine forever!

Jai Hind!

Vande Mataram!

# Preface

Bharat is not a piece of land; it is a living consciousness, a civilization which has survived the test of time for thousands of years. From the sacred hymns of the Vedas to the fearless resonance of freedom fighters, from the wisdom of the sages to the bravery of the warriors, each chapter in Bharat's history is an epic in itself.

This book is not a mere anthology of poems—it is a traversal of time, an ode to the spirit of Bharat that has not been broken through invasions, wars, and tests. Every poem in this book embodies a defining period of Bharat's history—whether it be the golden days of the Guptas, the unbreakable will of Shivaji Maharaj, or the martyrdom of revolutionaries like Bhagat Singh and Subhash Chandra Bose.

Why poetry? Because poetry is the soul's language—it can evoke feelings, inspire pride, and ignite the fire of patriotism. Through rhythmic poetry, I have attempted to awaken the valor, strength, and spiritual vigor that characterize Bharat.

This book is for every Bharat Bhakta, every history seeker, every poetry lover, and every dreamer who envisions the rise of Bharat as Vishwaguru. It is an assurance that the past of Bharat is great, its current is powerful, and its future is bound to glow.

Let me take you on this poem journey, Feel the thunder of warriors, listen to the teachings of saints, and behold the saga of Bharat's immortality!

Jai Hind!


— Hemant Avhad

# Acknowledgements

Composing this book has been a deeply inspiring and life-altering experience, and it could not have happened without the unstinting support, guidance, and blessings of so many.

I start with my respect for Bharat Mata, whose glorious history, vibrant culture, and unbreakable spirit have been the heart of this book. Every line written here is an humble obeisance to her glory.

I offer my sincerest thanks to the great saints, visionaries, and warriors of Bharat, whose wisdom and sacrifices have inspired and guided millions to date. Their heritage is the ground on which this book is based.

No such journey is ever undertaken alone, and I am most fortunate to have an amazing family that was with me, supported me, and helped create this book.

My wife, Sayali – My biggest strength and source of inspiration. Sayali, your unshakeable faith in my dream, your patience, and your unstinting support have been my biggest strengths. You have been my sounding board, my encouragement, and my partner in each step of the journey. This book is yours as much as it is mine.

My parents – The source of my being, my earliest gurus. Your principles, your sacrifices, and your love have molded the individual I have become today. The tales you shared with me, the teachings you imparted, and the tradition you inculcated in me have been the pillars of my passion for Bharat.

My in-laws – Your support, encouragement, and faith in my work have been treasured. Thank you for adopting my aspirations as your own and continuously pushing me to achieve higher things.

My brother, Nishal (Bhai) – You have been my biggest supporter and mentor. Your wisdom, your advice, and your faith in me have kept me grounded and motivated. Thank you for being there always.

My sister-in-law, Madhura – Your encouragement, kindness, and positivity have been an enormous source of inspiration. Thanks for being a part of my journey and constantly supporting me.

A Special Mention – Ishani (My Daughter)
The spark that lit the fire of my writing journey.It was not until Ishani came into my life that I found my real

calling as a writer and teller of tales. She presented me with a new viewpoint, a new purpose, and a new spark to share my thoughts in words. This book marks a milestone for me, and Ishani, you will always be the force behind the time I decided to tread this way.

To My Readers, a heartfelt thank you to the seekers, the patriots, and the lovers of Bharat, who have her greatness in their hearts. This book is dedicated to you. May it light the same fire of pride and love in you that I felt while writing it.

I thank poets, historians, and scholars as well for their works, which have helped me broaden my knowledge of Bharat's heritage and the struggles it has faced. Their words have been highly educative to form this book.

Finally, I thank the divine power, the invisible hand of fate, that made this book possible. Each word flowed as if directed by a power beyond me. This book is not only mine—it is of every Bharatiya who shares the faith in the greatness, strength, and timelessness of the rise of our motherland.

— Hemant Avhad

# 1. The Birth of Bharat - The First Dawn (~5000 BCE)

In the cradle of the Earth so wide,
Where truth and wisdom did abide,
The Vedas spoke, the hymns were sung,
A golden age had just begun.

Rivers pure and forests deep,
Sages woke from sacred sleep.
They sought the light, they found the way.
Their words still shine like dawn's first ray.

# 2. The Indus Valley - A Civilization's Might  (~3300 BCE - 1300 BCE)

By Sindhu's banks, a city rose,
With mighty walls and planned out rows.
Trade and art, so vast, so bright,
A beacon of the ancient light.

From Mohenjo-daro to Harappa's gates,
The past still speaks, it resonates.
A land of wisdom, vast and free,
A vision of prosperity.

# 3. The Vedic Era - Wisdom's Song (~1500 BCE - 500 BCE)

A fire burned, the Yajnas blazed,
The gods above, the men amazed.
In chants and shlokas truth was spun,
The age of Dharma had begun.

From sages deep in meditation,
Came the path of liberation.
In every mantra, every verse,
A timeless gift, the universe.

# 4. The Ramayana - A Tale of Honor (~5000 BCE, Treta Yuga)

A prince once walked through fire and pain,
For truth, for love, he broke the chain.
His exile long, his path was steep,
But Dharma's call he swore to keep.

In Lanka's halls, the battle raged,
The demon fell, the war was waged.
And when the dust had cleared away,
Truth and justice won the day.

# 5. The Mahabharata - The Battle of Fate (~3100 BCE, Dwapar Yuga)

Kurukshetra's fields ran red,
As warriors marched, as brothers bled.
The clash of arrows, shields, and steel,
The fate of kingdoms set to seal.

Krishna spoke, his words divine,
The Gita's truth, forever shine.
For Dharma stands, no fear, no plight,
For darkness falls before the light.

# 6. Chanakya - The Mind That Built an Empire (~375 BCE)

A scholar wise, a fearless guide,
Who saw the storm, who turned the tide.
He shaped a king, he forged a reign,
With mind so sharp, with thoughts so plain.

Against the mighty, bold he stood,
For Bharat's rise, for greater good.
His words of gold, his lessons bright,
Still shine today, a beacon's light.

# 7. Emperor Ashoka - From War to Wisdom (~268 BCE - 232 BCE)

In Kalings's dust, the bodies lay,
A king once fierce had lost his way.
The cries of war, the blood so deep,
Awoke his soul, he stood to weep.

He sought the path of peace and love,
With Buddha's light, he rose above.
No war, no chains, no needless fight,
Just Dharma's law and mercy's light.

# 8. The Gupta Age - The Golden Time (~319 CE - 550 CE)

A golden dawn, a scholar's dream,
The brightest minds, a shining beam.
Mathematics, art, and grand design,
The age of learning, pure, divine.

From Aryabhatta's guiding hand,
To poets crafting lines so grand,
The world beheld, they stood amazed,
At Bharat's light, its golden blaze.

# 9. The Rise of Chhatrapati Shivaji Maharaj (1630 CE - 1680 CE)

Through Sahyadri's peaks, a lion roared,
For Swarajya's dream, his sword implored.
A king who stood when all had kneeled,
A Maratha storm on battlefields.

A master mind, a fearless knight,
With honor pure, with will so bright.
His forts still stand, his tales still burn,
His name is one that shall return.

# 10. Chhatrapati Sambhaji Maharaj - A Martyr's Crown (1657 CE - 1689 CE)

The son of Shivaji, fierce and true,
His blood was bold, his heart so blue.
The Mughals came with chains in hand,
They sought to break, they made demand.

"Convert, or die," they dared to speak,
But not a word from him was weak.
He bore their torture, laughed in pain,
His name remains, his spirit reigns.

# 11. Maharani Lakshmibai - The Warrior Queen (1828 CE - 1858 CE)

Upon her throne, with steel in hand,
She vowed to save her sacred land.
With courage bold, with soul so free,
She roared, "I'll not give Jhansi away to thee!"

Through dust and war, she rode with might,
A blazing storm, a fearless knight.
Though fate did take her life away,
Her name still shines like dawn's first ray.

# 12. The Revolt of 1857 - The First War of Independence (1857 CE)

The bugles called, the swords were drawn,
The chains of rule would soon be gone.
From Delhi's gates to Awadh's land,
Each soul arose with fire in hand.

Mangal Pandey fired the first,
A spark of freedom, a nation's thirst.
Though crushed in might, it lit the way,
For India's rise another day.

**"1857 – The flame that refused to die!"**

# 13. Swami Vivekananda - The Voice of India (1863 CE - 1902 CE)

A monk once rose with fire in speech,
The world stood still, his words did teach.
"Arise! Awake! And know your power!"
Bharat's spirit, its golden hour.

He roamed the world, he spread the light,
Made Sanatan glow so bright.
His voice still calls, from past to now,
"Stand with faith, make fate allow!"

# 14. The Birth of Indian Nationalism (Late 19th Century - Early 20th Century)

Beneath the rule of iron and hate,
A storm arose, it questioned fate.
Tilak declared, "Swaraj is mine!"
Lal-Bal-Pal stood in a line.

With books and fire, they lit the way,
For Bharat's dawn, for freedom's day.
No longer slaves, no longer weak,
For every heart, for all who seek.

# 15. Bhagat Singh, Rajguru, and Sukhdev - The Martyrs of Freedom (1907 CE - 1931 CE)

They marched in light, they stood so tall,
The British feared their final call.
"Inquilab Zindabad!" they cried,
For freedom's cause, they lived and died.

The gallows came, yet none did shake,
With smiles they walked, with hearts awake.
Their death was life, their pain was pride,
For Bharat's flag, for those who died.

# 16. Subhash Chandra Bose - The Man Who Dared (1897 CE - 1945 CE)

A leader fierce, a will so grand,
He built a force, he made a stand.
"Give me blood, I'll give you free skies!"
The world now feared Bharat's rise.

From Berlin halls to Burma's fight,
His dream still shines, his voice still bright.
The war was lost, but not his dream,
His spirit roams in Bharat's stream.

# 17. The Quit India Movement (1942 CE)

"Do or die!" the father said,
And across the land, the fire spread.
The British knew, their time was through,
For India rose, for skies anew.

No longer slaves, no longer bound,
With cries so loud, they shook the ground.
And as the dawn of freedom neared,
Each voice declared, "No more we fear!"

# 18. August 15, 1947 - The Day of Freedom

The flags went high, the cheers so loud,
A nation free, a people proud.
From Nehru's voice, the words took flight,
"A tryst with destiny" burned so bright.

Yet wounds remained, the price was pain,
Partition's scar, the endless rain.
But Bharat rose, it healed, it grew,
With dreams so vast, with skies so blue.

# 19. The Future of Bharat - The Rise of a New Era

No chains remain, no fear at all,
For Bharat stands, forever tall.
A land of wisdom, fierce and free,
A beacon for eternity.

Its past is gold, its heart so pure,
Its future bright, its roots secure.
A world to lead, a voice so high,
The flag shall touch the endless sky!

# 20. The Rise of Modern India - A Nation's Renaissance (1947 CE - Present Day)

From humble roots, from wounds so deep,
A nation stood, refused to weep.
It built its roads, it touched the sky,
With heads held high, with dreams that fly.

From ISRO's launch to tech so vast,
From Chandrayaan to glory's past.
No land has grown with such great speed,
No spirit holds such fearless creed.

# 21. Bharat as Vishwaguru - The Future Beckons (The 21st Century and Beyond)

The time has come, the world must see,
Bharat's light shall lead the free.
Its roots so deep, its will so pure,
A guiding star that shall endure.

With yoga's peace, with minds so bright,
It spreads its glow, a golden light.
From Mars to trade, from words to steel,
Bharat's fate, the world shall feel.

"The rise of Bharat – The torchbearer of tomorrow!"

# 22. Vande Mataram - A Tribute to Bharat Mata

*(Written by: **Bankim Chandra Chattopadhyay** in 1870, from his novel **Anandamath**)*

वन्दे मातरम् - श्री बंकिमचन्द्र चट्टोपाध्याय रचित

**वन्दे मातरम्! वन्दे मातरम्!**
सुजलां सुफलां मलयजशीतलाम्,
शस्यश्यामलां वन्दे मातरम्!मातरम्।
वन्दे मातरम्! वन्दे मातरम्!

शुभ्रज्योत्स्नापुलकितयामिनीम्,
फुल्लकुसुमितद्रुमदलशोभिनीम्,
सुहासिनीं सुमधुर भाषिणीम्,
सुखदां वरदां मातरम्।

वन्दे मातरम्! वन्दे मातरम्!

This **immortal hymn** is not just a song; it is the **heartbeat of Bharat**, the **war cry of revolutionaries**, and the **sacred**

**chant of patriotism**. It inspired countless freedom fighters, including **Bhagat Singh, Netaji Subhash Chandra Bose, and Rani Lakshmibai**, and became the anthem of India's independence movement.

Let us remember the **sacrifices of our forefathers**, the **courage of our warriors**, and the **wisdom of our saints**—for Bharat is not just a land, it is a **living consciousness**, a civilization that shall shine eternally.